Level 4 is ideal for
read longer texts with
are eager to start rea

Special features

Full exploration of subject

Detailed illustrations capture the imagination

Air traffic control
Air traffic control is in contact with all the planes that are in the air.

Air traffic control has a control tower at the airport.

They have the flight plans for all the different planes, and they help the pilots to take off and land safely.

Longer sentences

Richer, more varied vocabulary

Cargo planes
Some pilots do not fly planes with passengers. Lots of aircraft fly around the world with different types of cargo.

Cargo pilots fly lots of different types of aircraft, all around the world.

Captions offer further explanation

It is important that the cargo lands on time!

Educational Consultant: Geraldine Taylor
Book Banding Consultant: Kate Ruttle
Subject Consultant: David Davies

LADYBIRD BOOKS

UK | USA | Canada | Ireland | Australia
India | New Zealand | South Africa

Ladybird Books is part of the Penguin Random House group of companies
whose addresses can be found at global.penguinrandomhouse.com.

www.penguin.co.uk   www.puffin.co.uk   www.ladybird.co.uk

First published 2019
002

Copyright © Ladybird Books Ltd, 2019

Printed in China

A CIP catalogue record for this book is available from the British Library

ISBN: 978-0-241-36112-2

All correspondence to
Ladybird Books
Penguin Random House Children's Books
80 Strand, London WC2R 0RL

I am a Pilot

Written by Simon Mugford
Illustrated by Joe Bucco

Contents

What pilots do	8
Passenger jets	10
Aircraft parts	12
In the cockpit	14
Aircraft crew	16
Flight plan	18
Air traffic control	20
Take-off	22
In flight	24
Time to land	26
Landing the plane	28

Pilot training	30
Cargo planes	32
Light aircraft	34
Helicopters	36
Rescue aircraft	38
Firefighting	40
A pilot's job	42
Picture glossary	44
Index	46
I am a Pilot quiz	47

What pilots do

Pilots fly lots of different types of aircraft. Flying an aircraft takes a lot of skill, and being a pilot can be a difficult job.

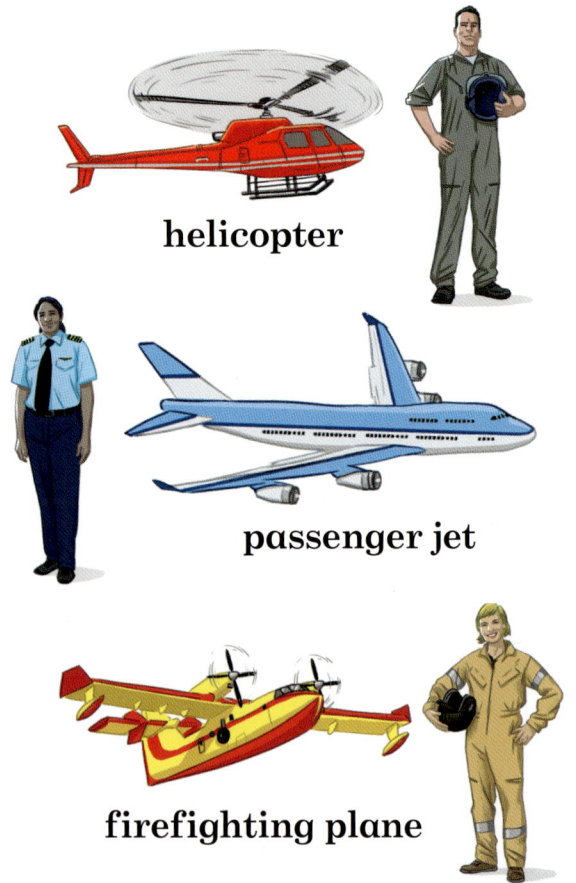

helicopter

passenger jet

firefighting plane

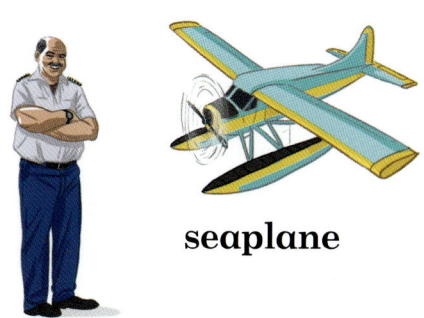

seaplane

rescue plane

light aircraft

All these aircraft have pilots.

Passenger jets
A passenger jet is a very big aircraft, and it takes lots of skill to fly one. The pilots are in charge of the safety of all the people on the plane.

Lots of people fly on passenger jets all the time.

Aircraft parts

These parts of the aircraft help it to fly.

Wings lift the plane into the air.

Engines move the plane.

In the cockpit

The pilots control the aircraft from the cockpit. A passenger jet cockpit has lots of controls, computers and instrument displays.

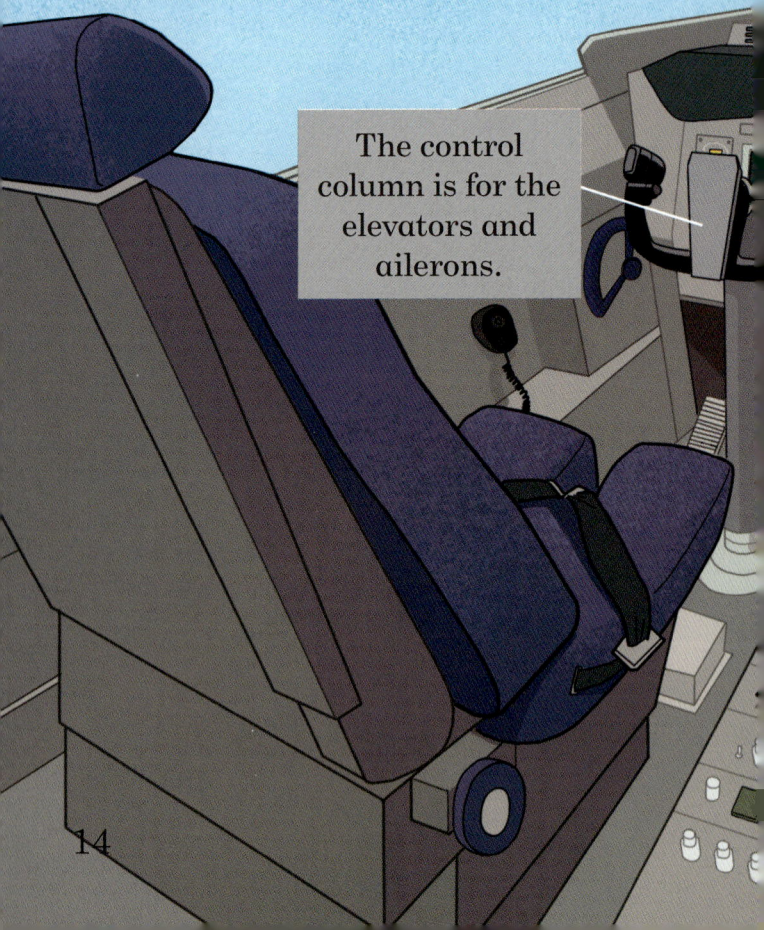

The control column is for the elevators and ailerons.

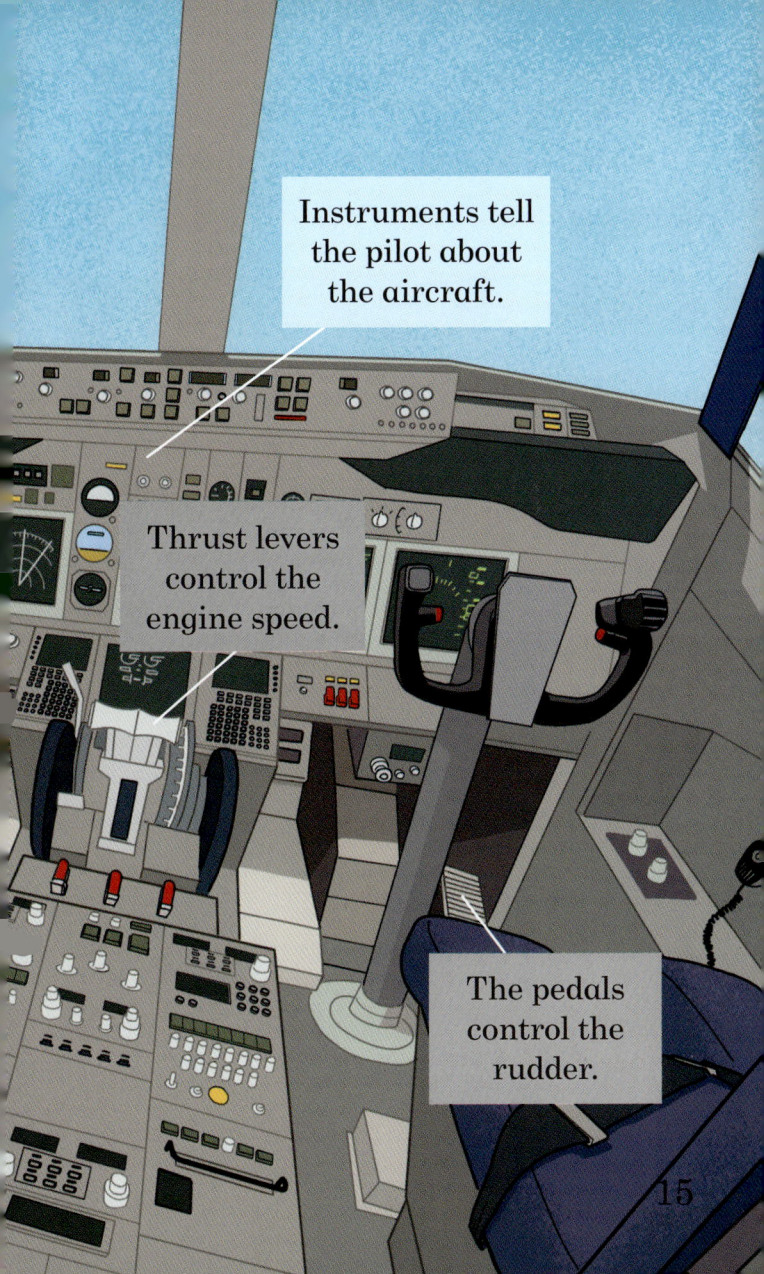

Aircraft crew

A passenger jet has two pilots – the captain and the first officer.

The captain is in charge of the plane.
The first officer helps the captain.

The cabin crew help the pilots and look after the passengers.

Flight plan

Before the plane takes off, the pilots make a flight plan. They check the weather and plan how much fuel to use.

The pilots check the aircraft's computers, instruments and controls, and do a flight-safety check with the cabin crew.

Air traffic control

Air traffic control is in contact with all the planes that are in the air.

Air traffic control has a control tower at the airport.

They have the flight plans for all the different planes, and they help the pilots to take off and land safely.

Take-off

It is time for take-off! Air traffic control contacts the pilots, and the plane moves on to the runway.

The thrust levers are pushed, and the plane moves forward.

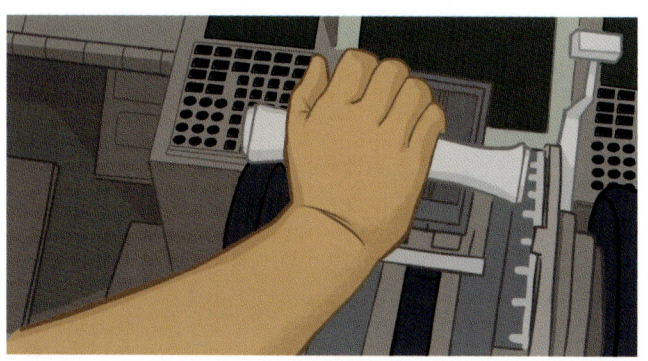

At the right speed, the captain pulls back the control column and the plane takes off.

In flight

When the plane is flying, it is controlled by a computer called an "autopilot", but the pilots are in charge! They check the flight plan, the weather and the instruments.

The captain tells the passengers about the flight.

The cabin crew look after the passengers.

Time to land

When it is time to land, the pilots take back control from the autopilot and contact the control tower at the airport.

The captain turns the plane to the airport and pushes the control column forward to make the plane go down.

Landing the plane

The pilots use the flaps and engines to slow the plane, and the first officer pushes a lever that puts the landing gear down.

landing gear

The pilot pulls back the control column, slows the engine, and lands the plane on the runway.

Pilot training

Pilots must train a lot before they can fly a passenger jet. They must have 1,500 hours of flying time.

Some pilot training is done in a flight simulator.

Flight simulators use computers to train pilots.

Cargo planes

Some pilots do not fly planes with passengers. Lots of aircraft fly around the world with different types of cargo.

It is important that the cargo lands on time!

Cargo pilots fly lots of different types of aircraft, all around the world.

Light aircraft

Many pilots fly planes called light aircraft. Light aircraft do not take many passengers, but are used for special jobs, like crop-dusting, or flying in air displays.

crop-dusting plane

These planes are flying in an air display.

Helicopters

Helicopters are a very different type of aircraft. They do not have wings, but they have rotor blades that turn to lift the helicopter into the air.

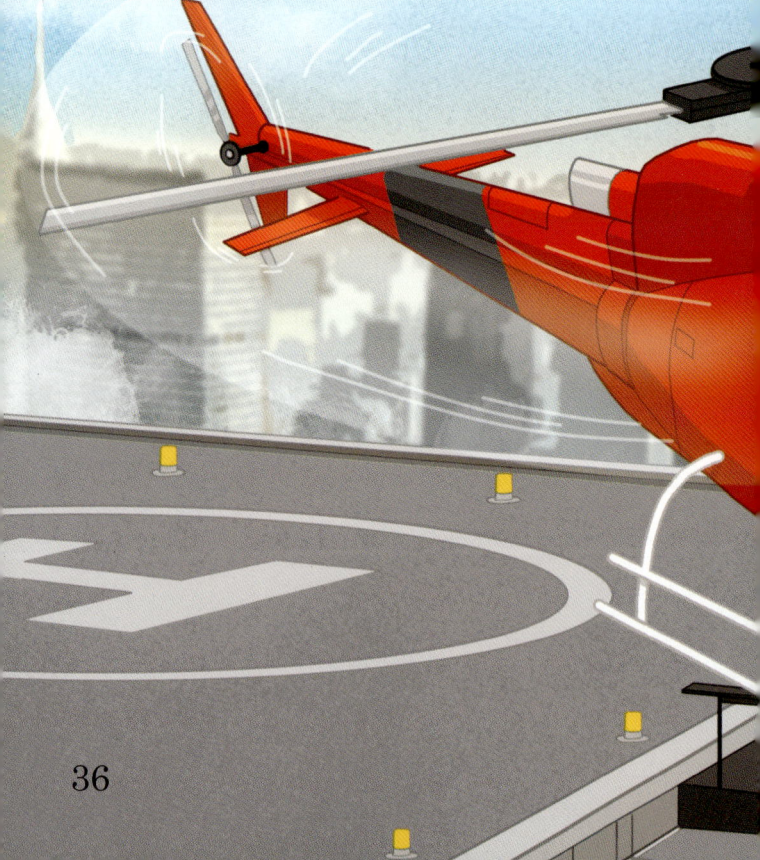

Helicopter pilots have different skills from other pilots, and they have special training.

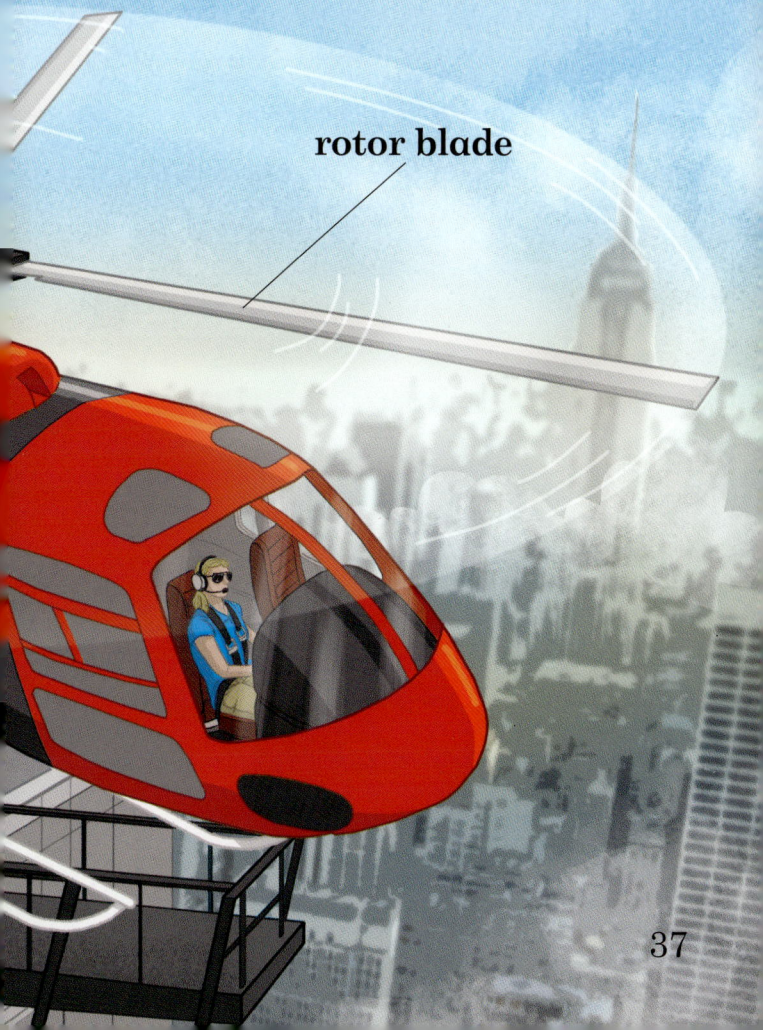

rotor blade

Rescue aircraft

Some pilots fly aircraft that rescue people in difficulty. Aircraft fly out to sea, and to parts of the land that are difficult to get to.

Rescue pilots have very special skills.

Helicopters are very useful aircraft for rescuing people.

Firefighting

Some pilots fly special planes and helicopters to put out very big fires. The aircraft take lots of water to the fire to put it out.

helicopter

Firefighting planes put out fires with water, like this.

firefighting

A pilot's job

Being a pilot is a very important job, but it can be difficult. Pilots get to fly all over the world, but they have to work many hours and are away from home for a lot of the time.

Picture glossary

 air display

 air traffic control

 captain

 cockpit

 crew

 firefighting aircraft

 flight simulator

 helicopter

 landing

 passenger jet

 rescue aircraft

 take-off

Index

aircraft	8, 9, 10, 12, 14, 15, 16, 19, 32, 33, 34, 36, 38, 39, 40
airport	20, 26, 27
air traffic control	20, 22
autopilot	24, 26
cabin crew	17, 19, 25
captain	16, 23, 25, 27
cargo	32, 33
cockpit	14
control tower	20, 26
firefighting	8, 40, 41
first officer	16, 28
flight plan	18, 21, 24
flight simulator	31
helicopter	8, 36, 37, 39, 40
land	21, 26, 29, 32
light aircraft	9, 34
passenger	17, 25
passenger jet	8, 10, 11, 14, 16, 30
rescue aircraft	38
take-off	21, 22